Marketing Faster Than a Lamborghini

by T.W.Flora

Table of Contents

1. Introduction
2. Chapter one- Pick your market
3. Get Noticed- Now!
4. How to maximize your social media!
5. Overcome yourself
6. If you can't beat them Join them
    6.1. Time for Getting some people to be your Haters!
7. Persistence Squeaky Wheel Gets the Oil
8. Other Business notes- Knowing that you don't know everything.
9. Reference page.

ISBN-13:
978-1974369171

ISBN-10:
197436917X

1. Introduction

Thank you for your Interest in marketing and sales. This book is a tribute to the old basics.

I will show you some of the things that I have observed from my marketing experience, sales, and what has worked for others. Even if you pick up one piece of advice, then it was all worth it.

Forget to try to sell something and Get up and Close that sells before you start a conversation!

2. Chapter one- Pick your market

Before you can market anything, you need to know what you are marketing.

So if you are trying to market the sales of a new shoe, then you figure out what the market is for shoes. Don't worry about advertising, or price or anything until you do this.

You should know everything about that product. How much it cost to make, how much it cost to sell. How long it takes to replenish. to ship. Competition for that product. Alternative products, what it sells for in the market and most importantly, **The Value of the product or service.** Patients and licenses.

The debate is that many people talk about competition and saturation of a product or service. You may be on the fence with the answer to this discussion.

There should be a standing factor when it comes to your product or service. I remember when Papa John's pizza came on the scene of a very competitive pizza market. The pizza is great, but that is not what caught people's attention in the beginning. They have adapted to the culture and is always trying new things to cut cost and new additions of products. I'm not 100 percent sure what made them better than Pizza Hut, or Domino's, at the time, but here are three things I remember about my first experiences with papa john's pizza.

1.) Value
2.) Taste
3.) That something Extra (Value part 2)

Explanation:

The cost of their pizza was $10 for a large Pizza; they had free delivery. The pizza seemed just to fill up the box, unlike the other two companies.
Taste in comparison to the top competitors at the time. They still have 100% customer satisfaction guarantee.

The pizza did not taste like eating the cardboard box with toppings.

That Something Extra; They added complimentary pepperoncini peppers and a Garlic butter dipping sauce. The Competition had only pizza in the box, but later they charged for the sauce.

The company now has added different sizes, wings, cookies and more. They dominate the advertising and marketing, and it shows. They became the official sponsor of the NFL, so they can actually say Super Bowl when advertising. Papa John's pushes pizza with every major sporting event. And sometimes blockbuster movies.

To the best of my knowledge, Papa Johns also push the envelope when it comes to cutting cost without touching the product. They invested in these WOW Ovens. They cooked the food at the same temperature of 500 Degrees. But it was able to produce more product with less time to make.

The old oven cooked pizza for about 9-10 minutes, but the Wow oven had two shelves of conveyors, and each one could cook the food in about 4.5 to 5 minutes. The new oven not only cuts the cooking time in half, adding the second convener doubled that time. The math is not 1 oven 10 minutes for a pizza to 2 ovens in 10 minutes could cook 4 pizzas. But the truth is that two pizzas can go side by side, so that in the same 10 minutes instead of cooking 2 pizzas, they now cooked 8.

As far as I know, they are the first one in the industry to cut the pay of its staff. I had worked there, and I was making more than minimum wage about 6.65 an hour. But when the federal minimum wage jumped up to $6.80 I was like, " this is nice!" and in few months when the federal minimum wage went up to the current $7.25, Papa john's said that they were cutting all of the drivers pay down to $4.00 per hour. The rate may be different depending on areas. They stated that it was like bartenders or waitresses. At the time my mom worked for pizza hut and a few months after that she told me that pizza hut was doing the same to their employees cutting long time benefits, closing sit down restaurants and also getting the WOW ovens.

Did you know that pizza as an industry has grown because of one company that dominated it? Domino's Pizza was once one store. The owners were struggling to make it for a while. One of the co-owners was delivering the pizza while the other one made the pizzas. He believed himself to be the fastest delivery driver ever. He began to tell people that he could get the pizza there in 30 minutes of less, or the pizza was free. What a deal? I could order a pizza, and if he doesn't bring it in 30 minutes I can eat for free! That is a major wow factor. That store's orders skyrocketed. They had to hire people to keep up with the number of orders. They had to expand their store to keep up with this demand. Now if you open up a phone book, pizza is under its own category, it is not listed under restaurants.

Pizza Hut is a sneaky one with their marketing. They will undercut on price for contracts. They will take a loss on a contract for today's orders of pizza to regain marketing on future pizzas. I remember as a kid when I read 5 books in class, and I had to write a book report on the books, I would then receive from the teacher a coupon for a free personal pan pizza. Of course, I was happy that I got an award for reading books. I mean who does that? I would go with one of my parents to the local Pizza Hut. But my mom or dad also wanted to eat so they would order a large and take home the rest. They also put up on the wall of the school and in the store your accomplishment. You become a great sales person for them, talking about what you did and talking about their pizza.
They also get many contracts with the government such as school lunches. So all of the hundreds of kids in the school eat Pizza Hut for lunch all of the time when they are not in the school and its Saturday night, what pizza are they thinking about? What company pizza comes to mind?

Remember people are creatures of habit. Ever sit in a particular area of a room? Ever go to a place to eat and even though there is a huge menu of things to try. You order from a small few items that you like from the menu. Have you ever bought the same or similar kinds of clothes? Do you ever hang out with the same kind of people? This does not mean that you cannot gain a new customer nor does it mean that you cannot lose a client that you have had for years.

When the iPhone 4 came out, the people that could not wait in line were the iPhone 3 customers. You could not give them a $1000 Android phone if you wanted to. Why? Because those customers had created an emotional attachment to the iPhone brand. Why did they? Because when Iphone2 came out, they began to market it as My iPhone. They built the emotional connection in the marketing.

It is just that people form attachments with items, people, companies and more, so use that knowledge to work for you. Push that connection, ask about that connection.

This is why car salespersons usually close the deal before you leave the lot. They begin to ask you about your life. With questions like, are you married? Do you have kids? What kind of car were you looking for? How much money were you seeking to spend? Do you have a car to trade in?

The whole time you are talking, you are building a connection with the sales rep. Since the sales rep seems to be listening to you about your life and they do a little talking. Then they have you pick out one from three cars like it is a game show. They even are calculating the trade into the price, if you have one. Then they kick it up a notch. They hand you the keys and have you sit in it. You are immersed into the product in a full sensory mode. You smell that new car smell. They move the sunroof back, they show you all of the storage compartments, they ask "you if you like music?" then they ask you your favorite radio station, and tune the car to your favorite station, while they go and copy your driver's license, they give you some time to think about it. You may even test drive two or three other cars, but the process will be the same. Most of this takes place before you even focus on the price. The dealer will get you excited about the car you told him that you wanted. Then he tries to help you get financing for it. He is now your friend. The dealer is the one you are rooting for to take your money! He usually will find a way to finance the deal. If not, then he will show you to their used car section and repeat the process with in-house financing. You came looking for a new car, and even if it is used you will leave with a car, usually.

That is the power of sales! In this case, the market was the dealer's lot, and the dealer dominated it. Your lot might be a flower shop or heating and plumbing van that can operate in any city. But you can only go so far. The more people you can reach the more you can sell.

If you have an online business, then the best thing to do is to maximize your expertise in that area. So if you sell Pokémon cards online. Then become the Pokémon, card expert. Put up 2 videos a day on YouTube about Pokémon cards. Post in Facebook, Twitter and the like. You need to Join every anime forum specifically targeting Pokémon cards. Write books about Pokémon cards, Go into mass chatrooms with discussions about Pokémon cards like Reddit. Talk about other bloggers who also share the passion, and become the authority on Pokémon cards.

3. Get Noticed- Now!

There was a story I once heard about two little girls setting up this lemonade stand at a park. They were there about 1 hour and not that many people were even noticing the stand, nor could they care about it. A third friend came over and said that she wanted to help. She began to yell at the top of her lungs, LEMONADE!!!! Then all of the kids kept screaming LEMONADE! After only a few minutes of this person in the park began to gravitate toward the lemonade stand. They ran out of lemonade three times. They kept sending the brother to get more lemonade and then they added more snacks. They had a great day, and they also learned the first thing about marketing.

You need to get the person's attention. If you do not have their attention, then you are not going to have them as a customer. Yell at them if you need to, say Hey man! Hey! Then complete the sale. You are going to get X number of widgets on Friday, and the cost is $45, sign here!

The Kardashians are masters of this rule. They make no products; they have no skills, yet they get your attention. They get your attention so much they are selling products by the millions just because they have your attention. I cannot think of any celebrity with less talent and more attention.

In the old days, there used to be a new boy on the corner trying to sell newspapers, yelling, Extra, Extra! Read all about it! Then They would yell out a Major Headline from the paper.

Newspapers are great at this approach. Headlines are never a complete sentence. They are designed that way to make the reader interested in the topic wanting more, even if that more is the rest of the sentence.

That is the nature of the news media. They report on disaster, murder, destruction and the like because when they report on these things, more people buy more newspapers, more people watch the news and the like. If you were them what would you do? You would put more of what the customer seems to want.

So do whatever you have to do to get people to notice you. I don't mean from a point of vanity but a position of admiration and respect. Johnny Knoxville and his friends from MTV show Jackass did very dangerous pranks, but it made them all millions of dollars, and now he is considered a legitimate actor.

When you need to put out your message or to get sales. One message stands out loud and clear

Keep asking until someone says "yes!"

4. How to maximize your social media!

Social Media is your friend. When it comes to sales, you cannot get a better source!

There are many ways that social media can help you sell. It is a tool, just like any other tool. If you think that you do not have time to post something, then think again. The cool thing about social media is that you can post one thing and then share it to all of your other social media.

For Example, you can put a post in Linked in and then share it on Facebook and Twitter with a push of a button. You can share a Tumblr post on a TSU and so forth. You can put a link to your main website in every post. It takes only a few minutes per day to post something to thousands of people.

If you do this 10 times a day, how many people will begin to see your stuff? I have a Friend, Matt Klingle of K studios. Check him out on Facebook.
https://www.facebook.com/klinglestudios/?surface=rese

This guy Matt worked in a factory; he has some insurance sales experience, but for some reason, he began to get the idea to become a professional photographer. He bought an expensive camera. He seeks out mentors. He went all over the place on his time off taking photos at events. He took photos for over a year and not getting any money from it. While at bars he began to photograph the bands that were playing. While other people would charge $300 or more per hour, he would charge whatever they would pay him, $50 here $100 there, many times for nothing.

One day he came to my house, and we talked about his branding and focus. He was already gravitating toward being around some crazy alternative bands. He would take some video of the band members; he has been paid to fly to other cities to shoot music videos which he also edited. I told him that he should work more with some mentors and other photographers so that he could learn more. I also directed him not just to take a photo but to create value for his customers. We talked about how he could target bands and venues to hire him. I told him that he was not actually making any profit. I said to him, Matt man if you are spending all day to make $100 and that is just what he does at the venue, he then has days of editing after that. He had concerns that people were taking his photos from the website and stealing them, and not paying him. I told him about how he needed to market his photos like the Grateful Dead band did.

Back in the early 70s and 80's, most bands were on stage. There was a separate section for mainstream media. The concert halls usually would say to the people in the crowd. " Attention Ladies and Gentlemen, please no recording devices or flash photography." The band and the record companies made money from the sale of records. They sold magazines, posters, and T-shirts at the concert. Only the newspapers and TV crews could take individual pictures or clips, and they were reviewed by someone before they could leave in many cases. They all had a fear of copy write steeling. Many Artist has to pay a lot of money for advertising the songs, the albums and selling tickets to the shows.

The Grateful Dead did not have a problem with selling out their concerts. They invited all of their fans to bring cameras, camcorders, tape recorders and the like. They would let them come to the front of the stage if they had a recorder. When John comes to the concert to hear his favorite band, The Grateful Dead he recorded it. Later John is making copies giving it out to his friends. He is playing the music everywhere he goes. He talks about how it is OK to copy the music and that the band wants people to share the music.

So now that John has shared this music with his best 3 friends, and they made 10 copies of the band's music, and the family members each make 1 copy for another friend of theirs and so forth. When The Grateful Dead came back to town, they already had a huge following of fans. They did not have to pay a dime for advertising. They charged premium prices for tickets. All of their shows were always sold out months in advance. So when the concert was there, they always went to the radio stations where they could meet with fans and talk live on the air. The DJ's became friends of the bands. They Even invited DJ's that were not Rock and Roll DJ's They would ask country music DJ's, Soul music DJ's and so forth. This created massive advertising with zero cost to them, while other bands had to pay promoters and radio stations and music stores to promote their albums.

Today with the invention of the Internet, your message can be seen by millions. There are so many people that get famous from videos that they post online, that you would not believe me if I told you. Justin Bieber was discovered beating his drums on a YouTube video. It is said that now there are more, people watching YouTube than all other TV and Cable TV combined. I don't know if that is true or not. You cannot argue that YouTube is free to publish. TV cost hundreds of dollars per city for a 30-second spot to run one time.

If a picture is worth a thousand words, then a video is worth a million.

So If you had a business and spent say $2,000 a month on TV adds. Cut it back to $500. Then pay your tubers that talk about your industry and find the ones with thousands of subscribers, and then pay them $100-$200 to make a few short videos promoting your product in the way they do. Almost instantly you would be put in front of over 100,000 people that are targeted to your kind of business. You do not have to build the following. They have done that! Use that to your advantage.

What if I have not money Troy? How can I start a business? First, build the following like the masters. Another great thing about YouTube is that there is a lot of expert advice. Yes, there is also a lot of noise. You can learn, even from the noise about what works and what does not.
Plus, you can see and hear the expert doing the task or goal. How amazing is that?

I know how easy it is to get caught up in the noise of social media. Give yourself time in your day for the noise. Like, give yourself 1 hour of posting things, to Facebook, Twitter, Google Plus and the like. Then give yourself 30 minutes to respond to others comments. Then move on to your projects of the day.

Market your things like Jay the lazy ass stoner! OK, he did not make up this way of marketing, but he explains it the best I have ever seen. I will break it down as short and sweet as I can. He talks about getting your website. In his case, he is a stoner and talks about selling bonds and other cool stuff. He would go to Google and type Google tagged cannabis. Then the top 3 to 10 people he sees is his focus. He begins at the top of the list moves down the list. If his # 1 person is Mr. Bong, then he follows everything, Mr. Bong. On Jay's website it might have a quick news article blog and within the blog, he places a few keywords and a few links to his affiliate sales of bongs. Now he has a place to put people; he began to go to his list of individuals. He Goes to Mr. Bong Tumblr. Jay then goes to all of the viral posts that Mr. Bong made. Then he follows all of Mr. Bongs Followers. Jay will reshare the followers viral post. He will comment on the follower's post. He will leave comments about his legalization of marijuana website and link that with many posts that he thinks people interested in marijuana. Jay will post tons of videos, pictures, infographics many with links back to his few main websites all about marijuana. On all of his main websites is his Hook. Bold, Visual Graphics with pictures of Bongs on them. People know where to get these awesome Bongs.

Setup Steps:

1. You Build a Connection
2. You Get their Attention
3. You Show your Value
4. You create the established connection by continuous posting, comments, and videos
5. You ask the customer for help. Hey man, help me out and subscribe, follow, share my stuff?
6. You Add more value. Show how you can solve some of their problems.
7. After they buy whenever possible follow up with the customer, that means so much for them.
8. With the follow up later send them an extra bonus.

OK so here is an example of an online only drop shipping business model that sells coffeepots as an affiliate marketer. You learned some tricks of the trade because you use a program like DS Domination, which I recommend. The best player in that game that I know has been breaking records. Vincent Harris my other income stream is traffic monsoon, and my site is www.americancaveman.com I have seen where he makes in months now with this what he did in years with DS Domination. Most people begin with DS Domination as a sort of boot camp for selling online. It is an excellent training program well worth the money.

You are Coffee Express Inc. In reality, you are Mr. Johnson from your couch in your pajamas. You have no product or store because you sell on a site like eBay. OK, so Mrs. Smith buys your red coffee express machine for $50. You let Mrs. Smith know that you agree with the price and shipping of only $10 and tax of $4.39 with a grand cost of only $64.39. She understood the price, shipping, and tax. She told you that at Walmart.com that same Coffeepot goes for $63, but they charge $12.95 for shipping. (Shows Value, You Have her attention, she is willing to pay that price)

So at this point your only communication is a text or email, stating that you received the order. By emailing her before and after the product was shipped with a quick note of thanks. Make sure to put the tracking number of the shipment right away. Later follow-up with a phone call and follow up emails with other products that she may like. She may want to try some of that Columbian super coffee bean that was in the news that cures cancer and you have some. After she pays you the $64.39 for the coffee pot, you see that on Amazon it is selling for $35.99 with free shipping, but you don't stop there. You find it at Overstock.com for $29.99, and they have a point program that you earn 5% on all coffeepots sold with free shipping. You then email her the tracking number. You also email her an eBook about coffee recipes and health benefits of Coffee. (you just added extra value after the sale) You could have ordered the item from Amazon and still sent a $2 coffee cup. Maybe one with your logos with a Thank you on it. (You just showed that more extra after the sale. You ask for a review. You make sure to ask if she wants a love coffee T-shirt. Ask if there is anyone else that might want one of your products. Many times you get things when you ask and put it in writing.

Become the Authority

I have made many mistakes along the way. But one Mistake that I did not do is began to write books. Every book I write adds to my list of authority to this site. I once heard a saying and as far as I can tell this statement holds true. " When something is in writing, people have a tendency to believe what is written down." We will go into to this more with SEO Later.

Since most people do not read books or that many books, they are not usually huge money makers. Books are great at showing that you are an authority on something. So if you are and auto mechanic, write a short book on quick fixes to things that you see every day. You will promote your book all over social media. The book may not sell but a few copies. But people are impressed that you took the time to make the book. You have something in writing that makes you look like an authority. You then you make YouTube videos that show the quick fixes. You let people know what you can do. You make videos with other people working on cars. You become the go-to guy for automotive repairs. The money will follow.

There was this custom car shop owned by Myles Kovacs. He loved customizing cars, and he was struggling to keep his business going. They have many magazines about cars. Myles had a particular fascination with giant rims on the cars. His favorite magazine at the time was Lowrider magazine. He noticed that they displayed many cars that looked great, but none of the magazines showed cars with big rims on them. There were a few, full-page full-color ads throughout the magazine that caught your attention. Myles did not understand why there were so many advertisements for big rims, but they never had cover stories about big rims on a car. So He created Dubs Magazine in 2000. There were a few celebrities that had come to his shop for some custom jobs. So when they did. He had them pose for him in front of their new giant rims. He pushed the magazine sales that showed people and celebrities and their rides showing new Dub rims on the cover. From the first issue, people began to take notice of his idea. Since he was the first he created the market, since he got celebrities, he did not have to pay them to take the photo. The celebrities were happy to take a picture with the new expensive custom rims that they just bought from the shop. Then because of all the self-made attention and magazine he greatly increased what he charges.

Tai Lopez has done the same with his platform. He puts celebrities in as many videos as possible. which has led to him being in more videos with more celebrities.

Maybe you are not from Hollywood, and you do not know celebrities. But thank god for social media because there are so many ways to reach out and contact them both directly and indirectly. I have spoken with a few celebrities and even have many follow my pages. It's a small world after all. Since they are following me, it would not be too difficult to send a message to them. Sometimes they respond back. To me, that is pretty impressive!

The more things that you produce, the more people you will be connected to. It's called the law of attraction.

5. Overcome yourself

You are your biggest enemy.

We all have fear. For you, the fear may be that you fail and cannot handle the embarrassment of that.

You know what is more embarrassing than that? Being a loser when you have the potential to become a great winner.

You will not try, weighing the fears over what more you could lose. I say, you are probably already losing or making just enough to get by. You do not feel happy that way either. So If you are already losing, and you might fail anyway, then why not do it. Why not reach higher than your dreams? If you jump but do not make it 10 feet, but you've done it 3 feet, then you have a 3-foot advantage over the other guy that did not jump.

We all have a weakness. The only way to overcome fear is with a plan. The plan may have practice in it. The plan may have a number in it. You do not like cold calling people, good get on the phone and call 100 people today, then 200 tomorrows, and so on. How many calls before you are no longer scare to dial that phone?

Every expert in the history of time had practiced their craft until they got better, and you can too.

6. If you can't beat them Join them

I saw the power of this step when I was selling a book called. The 67 Steps: The Easy way to the Good life. I even told people that Tai Lopez inspired it. I found a hole in one of his marketing. I see marketing gaps, and I filled that hole. He had many links that he paid to drive traffic to Amazon. He did this as a marketing funnel. For example, people see a tweet that he posts with a link to Amazon. The person clicks the link and goes to a page where Tai Lopez had a free app to download to your phone to get his radio show. The whole time Tai Lopez promotes his products and services on his main website. Tai Lopez did not have a 67 steps book. So I wrote it, I made it a quick reference guide to his 67 steps video program. Even though I had my name right on the cover of the book, it quickly began to rank higher and higher on google and amazon that his guru book did on Amazon. Many times, I found it so funny that when you type in the words in the search bar, " Tai Lopez books,", "Books by Tai Lopez", "The 67 Steps book by Tai Lopez" that my reference guide was usually at the top of the search results, even though my grammar was not so great. I had many spelling errors, and I even had some horrible reviews. I did have more positive reviews than negative ones until I got into a copyright battle with him about content. But that did not stop him from liking me so much he let me become an affiliate marketer for him. If you want to check out his powerful program, follow my link.
http://www.the67steps.com/c/troyflora /

I have since repeated this process. The awesome thing is when other companies have paid advertisements to sell your product. When I write books and want to sell them, I, of course, I will promote my books, but I am not the only one to promote them. I used Createspace for my self-publishing company, and they promote on Amazon, Barnes&Noble and about 20 different sites I never even know about. Amazon has versions of its website in many countries. From the example I gave about Tai Lopez, I would frequently see a sponsored ad ran at the top of Google from Barnes and Noble and more visually showing the book. Sometimes the automated Google voice would read off the title for me. I never spent a dime on one Advertising.

I have done this many times over. Try it and you too will be amazed how to rank high on the searches. If you do pay for advertising, it might be easier to use a smaller search like Bing that charges less to advertise. Google ranks according to many factors. If you are ranking high on Bing, then, in turn, you will rank high on Google.

Here is how Google works, in one word, relevance.

In the old days, it may have been more about placing keywords. I even heard of websites with a million keywords on them just to make them rank high. Those days are gone! The web crawling spiders shift through the information and categorize how valuable that information is.

The Story of Google.

Google began in January 1996 as a research project by Larry Page and Sergey Brin when they were both Ph.D. students at Stanford University in Stanford, California. Sergey Brin has this crazy idea back then. He said that he wanted to copy the entire world wide web onto his desktop PC. That even sounds like a crazy idea today. He began downloading a copy of every website he found. He was on a mission. When the memory began to fill up on the hard drive, he networked it into another hard drive. You can go to Google wiki and see a picture of the first tower they had like 20 hard drives stacked on top of each other from the floor to the ceiling. They began to have networks of hard drives going all down the hallway, and there were wires all over the place. Now at the time the conventional search engines ranked results by counting how many times the search terms appeared on the page. Alta Vista was king of search at the time. Alta Vista stated that their search was so powerful that it equaled searching through a stack of papers to the moon and could find that key work in 30 seconds. The two theorized about a better system that analyzed the relationships between websites. They called this new technology PageRank; it determined a website's relevance by the number of pages, and the importance of those pages, that linked back to the original site.

Page and Brin originally nicknamed their new search engine "BackRub", because the system checked backlinks to estimate the importance of a site. Eventually, they changed the name to Google, originating from a misspelling of the word "googol", the number one followed by one hundred zeros, which was picked to signify that the search engine was intended to provide large quantities of information. Originally, Google ran under Stanford University's website, with the domains *google.stanford.edu* and *z.stanford.edu.*

What they did was create a Dewey decimal system for the Internet. They tried to sell it to all the major portals at the time as an extension app for the portals. Believe it or not, they were turned down by all of the players, Lycos, Altavista, Yahoo, America Online, etc. You may ask

Why would anyone turn down such a powerful tool? At the time, if you were on Yahoo or AOL then they wanted you to stay on their website. I am Joe Smith; I am a Huge fan of Yahoo! I Go to yahoo for my news, my videos, my Yahoo chat rooms, my email is Joesmith@yahoo.com. I spend hours playing on the online games area. Yahoo puts up flash advertisements. Yahoo had Big Colorful Banner Ads. If Yahoo makes money from the sponsors that put ads on the website, and because you spend hours of your day on the website, you will see those advertisements over and over.   This is how Yahoo makes money. Why would Yahoo want you to leave their excellent website? The wouldn't, and they didn't. All of the Portals thought that the Google tool was the worst thing they could have at the time. Where is Alta-Vista Today?

Yahoo remains because they later made a deal to work with Google as an affiliate and incorporated the Google search bar into their website that earns money for both. Now any website can do the same and make money from Google ads as well. So Thank Yahoo for the Google search bar in other sites.

"If you cannot beat them, join them" is a saying for a reason.

Now that you know how Google works you can milk it for what it is worth. If people see an advertisement on Facebook, they might look at it and say, I might check it out later. But when people are searching in a search bar, many more people are looking for something to buy with a credit card in their hand. If you get their attention in the search bar, then you are much more likely to get their money.

But I have been blogging all day, and I cannot get one sale.

You need to have relevance, but you also need to link with Authority sites. There are many Authority sites that you can get for free and post for free and link those back your main website.

So if you sell skateboards. You have a website called MegaSkater.com where you sell all kinds of boards and accessories. You only have $100 for your entire web budget. You just spent half of that on the domain name, hosting and your WordPress blog. You started to post blogs on blogger.com, and you went to a few smaller skater forums. So far all of your efforts have not been much.

Here is what you do. You get off your lazy butt and get very active. Make your activity highly focused. Every day post 5-10 short 2-3 minute videos about skating. Post 1 video about a new skateboard and its features. Post the video to all of the social media, Facebook, Twitter, Tumblr, Reddit, Pinterest, Instagram, snap chat, and more. That will take you about 1 hour a day. Many times you can link accounts together and post to three at the same time. You then spend another 30-60 minutes a day sharing other people post. I think the most efficient way to do this is to answer questions on video. Then post that video everywhere. After you have 1000 videos, how many people do you think will be following you? I had about 10,000 followers without any video in 6 months. As soon as I began to post videos. Those numbers Jumped.

If you are even more lazy, to make your own videos, then you can keep sharing already viral videos and put those on your blog sites with links back to where you sell the skateboards. You just found a video where Tony Hawk just broke a world record, and the video already has 56 thousand shares. You Post this video to all of your social media with a link back to your skateboard website. Check out the new Rockerboard the same one that Tony Hawk uses! Just like the movie Field of Dreams " If you build it, they will come."

Last note on all of your videos asks people to help you out, share the video, like the video and reply to the video. This builds your connections and credibility. Within a few months, you will be making many more skateboard sales.

For more tips and tricks check out my account on Facebook, Tumblr, Twitter, Linked in, and YouTube. Name; Troy flora

Michael Cardone one of the best salespersons ever stated that if you want to make more money, you need more haters. He said if he has 10,000 haters he's making a million dollars.

The more I thought about his message and the more that I have related it to any success that I have ever seen. This statement if so very true. The more people that hate you, the more successful you will be. This goes against what we are taught. We are taught to be nice and don't fight your brother, don't touch that light socket, don't do this and don't do that to be nice. Even when inside your head you are screaming, you have to pretend that you are not, to be nice.

He was not saying not to be kind to people he was saying that you should not pretend to be something that you are not. Many time when it comes to business you have to be not so nice, but it does not mean that you are unkind. If you have 10 employees but you have had a huge loss in business, you may have to let 3 people go. It does not mean that you are angry with them, it may not even be that they do a bad job, it's just business. It is what it is, business.

I once heard a story about the radio DJ Howard Stern. This guy has an awesome story. He is not known to be a very attractive person; He is known for saying the most outlandish things on the radio. He talks about sex, drugs and everything under the sun in a very vulgar manner. Most people who are radio station DJ's do not become rich.

After many years, of some success, he wrote his life story in a book that was made into a movie called private parts. This added to his credibility even though his television show was canceled. He was making millions because of the followers that he had built up and his wild reputation. There was a survey that was conducted to see how they could improve the show. From the random surveys that were done the results were impressive. The people that were his fans, the people that said they loved Howard Stern stated that they would listen to his radio show for about 1 hour a day. They were asking why did they listen to him for 1 hour when there is so much out there on the radio. Their response was that they would continue to listen to him to see what crazy thing he would say next. The people in the survey that claimed that they hated Howard Stern would tell the surveyor that they would listen to him for 3 hours a day. They were asking why did they listen to someone that they hated for 3 hours a day when there is so much out there on the radio. Their response was that they would continue to listen to him to see what crazy thing he would say next.

Howard Stern did not change a thing with his show. The haters talked about him all of the time. They were his best advertisers. When XM radio was first begging, they wanted some big DJ's to put shows on the air. They agreed to a few million in the contract with Howard Stern. When it came time for the contract to be renewed they could not pay Howard Stern his asking price. So they paid him a huge chunk of money, they paid him more in XM radio stock. He is one of the principal stockholders of XM radio and is worth over 1 Billion dollars. Not bad for a DJ with a lot of haters.

7. Persistence Squeaky Wheel Gets the Oil

Bill Gates stated that for 10 years he did not take a day off from work, for years he paid his employees in stock because he could not give.

Colonel Sanders when he began, did you think that he was rich? Nope, he saw his social security check which was only a couple of hundred dollars and said " I can't live on this" He did not have many resources. He did not have much money. He did not have any other retirement saved up. He did not have much at all. All he had was a chicken recipe that a lot of people liked. That was it for him. He could not even get a small business loan to get it off the ground to sell it. Poor Col. Sanders. Even though he was not that smart, he used the only idea that he had to try to make some money with it.

He went to the first mom and pop restaurant. Remember, he was an old guy with a white beard, and he wore an all-white suit. He walked into the place and said "Hello, my name is Colonel Sanders, I have the best chicken recipe in the entire world. I want to give it to you for free. All I want is for every time you sell a piece of chicken you pay me a small portion of the proceeds for the rest of your life." What do you think the owner of the place said to him? Do you think that he said, " Oh boy, I have been waiting for you my whole life"? No, He said, "Sir, your brain is fried." Who do you think you are with the white beard and suit. Santa clause in the summer time? I've got my chicken recipe, I sell my chicken, get out of here old man!

How many times do you think that he failed before he succeeded? 1009 times he got an NO before he got his first Yes. How many of you would stop after 500 NO's and think well maybe I need to recheck my recipe? But because of his persistence he revolutionized the way we eat. Today food franchises are everywhere.

Les Brown tells a story of how he wanted to be a DJ with a local radio station. He went up there to get a job. The manager in charge told him that there were no jobs available. He went back the next day and said Sir are there any jobs available? The manager said " I told you yesterday we had no jobs. Les said, well maybe somebody got fired? The manager said, " nobody got fired we have no jobs." Les left and came back the next day. He said to the manager, hi sir; this is Les Brown again, are there any jobs available? The manager annoyed replied, look, son, I told you there were no jobs available. Why do you keep coming back? Les Brown said well sir, maybe someone got fired, or maybe somebody died; you don't know. The manager replied nobody died, nobody got fired, there are no jobs available. Les Brown left and came back the next day. Hi Sir, remember me? The manager asked, what can I do for you, Les Brown? Sir do you have any jobs available? The manager again said, No Mr. Brown we do not have any jobs available? Les Brown said well I just thought maybe if someone did not show up? The manager said everyone showed up. This goes on for another week or two and then Les Brown again comes into the studio and asked if there were any jobs available? The manager at his wits end from annoyance said to Les Brown? Why do you keep coming here? Les Brown said, well sir as you know, all I want is to be a DJ here at the greatest radio station in the world, I just keep thinking that maybe somebody won't show up either by being fired, or quit or if they didn't show up. The manager said get me a Coffee. Les Brown said " Yes sir, right away. He became a sort of an unpaid assistant for some time. Every opportunity to learn something from everyone in the building he took. Les Brown talked to all the DJ's, the sound techs, the custodians, the receptionist and so forth. Les Brown was like a sponge for radio. He studied the and took notes on how the controls worked and he practiced being a DJ while at home in front of the mirror. He waited patiently for months. He said then one day his opportunity had arrived. One day this DJ who liked to drink, he was called ROCK, he had way too much of the sauce one day was not doing a good job, saying things that were inappropriate for the air and such. Les was watching and in his head saying, go on drink rock drink. The phone rang, and Les picked up and said hello. It was the station manager. He told Les that rock needed to get off the air, but he told Les to call one of the other DJ's to see who could come in to finish Rock's shift. Les said, Yes Sir! But he did not call any of the DJ's he called his mother and his sister and said," mama, sis, turn on the radio because I am about to go on the air!" Les then called back the manager and said:" Sir I could not get a hold of anyone!" The manager said " OK Les just get the rock out of there and don't say anything, just play music until I can get somebody there. Les Brown Said "I will do the best I can sir" He hung up, and Rock was about passed out on the air, Les slid rock to the side and then spoke up as perfect as he ever did, " Alright everybody this is the power of Les Brown bringing you great hits and smooth jams, here is one of my favorites by (some artist) then the music played. After about 1 hour the manager called back and told Les just to keep doing. He was very popular and became a regular paid DJ.

Michael Jordan rode the bench the first two years of his high school basketball team, and one time was cut from his team because he was too small for the game, but by the time he was in the senior year he was becoming a great player. From practicing every day.

Charles Shults (Peanuts comics) was turned down for a job by **Walt Disney,** who was fired for lack of creativity in his early career at a newspaper they told him that he was "Lacking Imagination" and "Having no original ideas."

Albert Einstein was expelled from school. When he was 4 years old before he began to speak and his teachers said that he would never amount to much.

Marilyn Monroe was dropped from her first movie contract because she could not act and was not pretty enough.

Isaac Newton failed miserably when he was put in charge of the family farm, so his uncle took charge and sent him to Cambridge where he finally succeeded.

Abraham Lincoln's Famous Failures
1832 Lost Job
1832 Defeated for legislation
1833 Failed in business
1834 Elected Legislature
1835 Had nervous breakdown
1838 Defeated for Speaker
1843 Defeated for nomination for Congress
1846 Elected to Congress
1848 Lost Renomination
1849 Rejected for land officer
1854 Defeated for Senate
1856 Defeated for nomination for vice- president
1858 Again Defeated for Senate
1860 Elected President

Elvis Presley was fired by the manager of the Grand Ole Opry after just one performance and was told: "you ain't going nowhere son, go back to driving a truck."

Oprah Winfrey - Was demoted from her job as a news anchor because she "Wasn't fit for television".

Steve Jobs - At 30 years old he was left devastated and depressed after being unceremoniously removed from the company he started.

Marshal Mather's AKA **Eminem** - A High School Dropout, whose personal struggles with drugs and poverty culminated in an unsuccessful suicide attempt.

Thomas Edison - Teacher, told him he was " too stupid to learn anything, and he should go into a field where he "might succeed by his pleasant personality."

The Beatles - Were rejected by Decca Recording Studios. Who Said "We don't like their sound...They have no future in show business."

Dr. Seuss - His first book was rejected by 27 Publishers.

Winston Churchill -British Prime Minister -His parents ignored him. He did poorly at school. He stuttered and spoke with a lisp. They called him a disappointment and a boy of "Low intelligence."

We could go on and on.

"Courage doesn't always roar. Sometimes courage is the little voice at the end of the day that says I'll try tomorrow" - Mary Anne Radmacher

Never give up! Never! If what you are doing is not working, you can try something else. You can change it but do not stop trying.

If you've never failed, you've never tried anything new

8. Other Business notes- Knowing that you don't know everything.

Knowing that you don't know everything.

Sam Walton stole ideas from what his competitors did and adapted the lessons from his competition and integrated it into his own company, Walmart. The innovation of Walmart came from him streamlining his entire business. He had a few stores that were just as struggling as his completion. What he did was instead of hiring trucking companies, he just bought trucks and created a trucking hub and then he moved his goods from store to store. Since he did not have to pay the profits from the other contracted shipping middlemen. He saved money. Then he was able to do what the other companies could not. He could lower to cost of all of the goods in the store. Because of how he cut the shipping cost down. His completion could only lower their prices so much. The more stores that Walmart created, the more shipping and holding that was created.

Sam Walton himself remained humble. He drove an old truck to work and did not flaunt his money. Sam Walton was in a constant state of improving his business. He started with one store, and now Wal-Mart is a worldwide success with no end in sight.

Abraham Lincoln- "I Learned from everyone I meet, though often it is what not to do."

Write down your goals, and write down all great knowledge you get from anyone you meet.

Also, it's like learning vocabulary, by repeating it.

Turning a Lump of Coal into A Diamond

Delay current pleasures for the future ones. You take steps today so the future will be better. This goes back to the Michael Jordan 1000 shots to get it right or like Arnold Schwarzenegger did 1000 reps to build up the muscles to become Mr. Olympia.

You need to push through the pain in order to have gained.
One spotter was yelling motivation at you.
He said "come on! You are already in pain, get a reward for your pain!"

This is also known as developing a thick skin. Go through the pain to make yourself stronger.

When I was in the army, there was a particular day when things were not going right. Anyone in the military will tell you things change all the time and many times information is confusing when orders change and everyone does not get the order or when orders conflict.

One day while I was in the army, this was not in a war zone at the time, it was in the States at a base. We were at Fort Hood, Texas when my squad leader said something that just brought the years of complaining into full perspective. He said that the whole thing was F'd up and chaotic for a reason. I asked him what reason could it be to have everyone confused and conflicted? He said it was the wisdom of the leadership. He said our leaders might look like they have their head up their butts. However, that is not the case. Then he completed the thought as we joked about the chaos in the motor pool.

He said "Things are all messed up and chaotic in peacetime over and over again that way when we are in war, in some other country, and things are really fucked up and chaotic that we will all be just used to it, and it won't matter, we will say oh well, here we go again and move on."

That just made so much sense about so many things.

In the military, we say that these things build character.

There was a story of a tree that falls into a swap. As the tree falls deeper into the bog and gets buried deeper and deeper, this tree begins to change chemical form. At first, the outer part that protects the tree (it's skin) begins to deteriorate, but the core of the tree under all of that weight, heat, and pressure begins to change and get petrified hard. At first, it becomes like hardwood or like a rock. But it does not stop there. Under more weight, heat, and pressure over time becomes a diamond, one of the hardest substances on the planet.

I even heard of a woman named Glynis Barnett turning her dead husband into a diamond.

Recap- deteriorating soft and wet wood, solidifies to rock like structure- to a Diamond!

The Diamond is 10 times as hard as the tree ever was.

People are the same. We say we want it easy, but when it is difficult, it makes the next time easier, and we are stronger for the experiences. Like me in the past, I embrace even the bad times with the knowledge of the difficulty to make the next time better.

Manage Your Destiny

This chapter is about matching your signature strength with what you are pursuing. Many times you hear about this in Hollywood. A person asked you what you do. You state that you are an actor or actress, but mainly you are a waiter or a waitress. This is a mix match of what you are pursuing.

There are many great actors that in their early careers did other jobs. That is not what I am talking about. It is the core of your destiny. Look at Danny DeVito for example. A great actor but, when he was starting he literally went to every audition. And I mean every audition. Hundreds if not 1000s auditions. For a long time, he was horribly rejected. No offense to Mr. DeVito, because I love most of his work. But he was told the following; "Get out of here. You are fat, ugly, and going bald". He was not what you think of as Hollywood premium material. But his persistence paid off. Eventually, he began to get secondary roles. He was well liked by people on the set both on and off camera. That began to be noticed. His roles in movies and shows began to expand. The rest is history.

Even when he was working other jobs to survive. His spirit and core were an actor long before he got his first job as one. He never said he was trying to be an actor. He told everyone he was the best actor!

Recommended reading the book

Managing Oneself (Harvard Business Review Classics) 1st Edition

Here is a link to it. http://amzn.to/1lEGGaB

Don't Wait for luck, Make Your Luck

In the book, *The Richest Man in Babylon*, there is a great discussion on what makes people rich.

They have many discussions. One was about winning riches at the gaming tables. It was an open forum where many men in the group were allowed to speak. They would ask the richest man in the city how he became rich and if it was something that could be learned.

The techniques are timeless and are definitely something that any one person could learn to do and could be taught to any other person. With time, patience, and the wisdom to seek opportunities when they come by.

Tai Lopez refers to his time with the Amish as a time where money was not that important. Everyone works for the community. They have a day off for rest and not much use for vacation. Most other people look forward to their precious time off whether it is a federal holiday, paid time off from work, leave, or just the weekend. We all work for the weekend. He calls this a vacation mentality.

To go back to the richest man in Babylon story where the men inquire about the sudden gain of riches such as luck at the gaming tables. Arc-had asked anyone in the group if they have ever been blessed by the goddess of luck. But only one man stated that he had ever won in the gaming tables or at the horse track. That same man stated that over time he had lost 3 or 4 times what he won at gambling. So the story goes that no one wins at the games. Even though they had all heard of people who had sudden wealth come to them, it brought them much more disparity than prosperity because they did not know the value of it, how to protect it, and their own interpretation of their wealth and belief of the wealth. That is why they continued with great lessons on how to keep it, value it, protect it, lend, loan and give it away. Most importantly how to make their wealth grow.

They later get into more discussion of luck that almost came, but they were too blind, stupid, stubborn, or ignorant to see the opportunity that slipped through their fingers. One trader gave a great example when he was locked outside of a great city. The walls were secured from a great attack. It was very dark. Many traders were waiting for the morning to come, for the walls to open up to trade at the market. The man continued, this guy from a faraway city was there to trade. He was going to give me 500 of his sheep for 1/2 price if I could only give him 2/3 of that 1/2 price now and he was going to leave a small group of his slaves a hand behind while he could head back as fast as possible for his ailing family member. But it was very dark, and the group of animals was vast and moving, it was too difficult to count and verify the deal. I knew it was a great opportunity; I just did not follow through. Anyway, he left anyway and his small employment stays with instruction to get a fair market price and come home as quickly as possible.

In the morning, when the gates opened up, the market merchants had been walled in, and their supplies were very low. They were paying 3 times as much per sheep head and any other supplies because of cost going up from supply and demand. The next day the cost was back to normal price, and the man had missed a great opportunity. This was also luck, but he ignored it.

They cover many examples like this in the book. The point is to have the wisdom to see opportunity when it comes and take action to seize it.
It is not enough just to see the luck but to create situations that it will be counted on.

Many people call it a plan, or a plan of action.

You can make your own luck. If you are in debt, or you are behind on a bill, you cannot say things like, "I can't afford it." You need just to reword it a little. Say "How can I afford it?" The difference is in the action. When you say "I can't afford it," that is the end of the thought process in your head. Nothing more to think about. You cannot do it. But when you say " How can I afford it?" your mind begins to go into overdrive. You will be bombarded with many ideas on how to make it happen. You will see the possibility on how you can afford it. Then find the best action plan.

Remember this is a very big world and there is always a way to make something happen.
You do not have the money but, someone in the world does.
You may not have the knowledge but, someone in this world does.
You may not have a plan but, someone in this world does.
You may not have the connection but, someone does.
You may not have the resources but, someone does.

And if you are determined then you will do it no matter what.

Proof scenario; let's say you have an only child that is dying or a rare disease, and you had 30 days to come up with $20,000 to save his or her life. Would you save your child's, life? Without question, anyone would say, " I would do anything to save my child's life" And they would. So why to wait for death at the door. Just do it.

To make your luck happen does not have to be dramatic. You do not have to quit your job if you don't want to. You could make small changes each day. If you have to make 3 sales, then make 4 or 5 or 10. That added up will eventually show that you are bound above others. Even one extra sale a day would be 200 or 300 more a year. What manager would not recognize that kind of contribution or company? I once worked a Liberty Tax cooperate office where I would meet their minimum requirements and throughout the day I was given leeway to work on another project. I was creating connections and projects with outside agencies. Eventually, I had to cut my employment down to working a few hours one day a week, by my choice, they were happy to have me work there even one day a week, due to my contributions to the company. Even later when I had to quit the job, entirely I was told that I would always have an opening at Liberty tax, even if that call center department closed down. I only worked there a few months. But I made a lasting impression.

You could eventually work toward your goals. It does not have to be a, "I'll do it later,": but more like I'm working toward it now.

Three types of people

1- People who make things happen.
2- People who watch what happens.
3- People who wonder what just happened.

An entrepreneur remakes the world in his own image. -Alan Nation

Like Richard Branson was on an island after a hurricane trying to get out. There were no flights out. So he got the idea to rent a plane and sold out the seats. This was the seeds of the idea for later Virgin Airlines.

To be creative and skilled.

Let say you like basketball. You don't have to be a player; you could be an owner. You could be a vendor. You could even be a custodian to get access to the stadium and network within. You use whatever you can at the time and then grow from there.

What would the world around you as far as health goes?
What interests you when making money?
What group socially would you like to be a part of you?
What is outside of yourself, your charity or church?

The process of the life is to make the life.

If you have a great Idea for an invention but you do not have the resources to make or manufacture it. Then get it patented and sell out the rights. Don't worry that is your only idea. When you start getting royalty checks, your mind will be working on the next big idea.

Get Out of the Darkness- Self Assessment

Look at your body, love life, or finances the way you want them to be.

What is the path to what you want and are you walking toward the right path to your goal?
The straight path to your goal.

What is the path to the solution that you want?

7 scientific processes to yourself.
Actions toward your goal.

1. Ask yourself a question.
Example: How do I get into better shape?

2. Research the possible answers.

3. Make a hypothesis (If I do this, that will happen)

4. Test- try and do it.

5. Observe the results that you get.

6. Analyze the results to see if it is working.

7. Get advice from somebody to see if you are doing the right thing.

Repeat the process. If it is not getting you toward your goal, stop doing it and try something else.

Do not just stop on your goal just that activity that is not working.

Thomas Edison tried over 1000 times to create a light bulb. After 5 or 10 times would you have quit. Persistence is not failure; it is just a step on the way. He was determined to find a filament that worked. When he tried something that did not work, he wrote down the results. So if he tried horse hair, and it burned up, he wrote down horse hair burned 20 seconds. Then he would try banana leaves, then corn husk, then piano wire, and so forth. He did not keep working with horse hair. But he did continue his search for a long burning filament for his bulb. Thank god because now we have many forms of electricity and electronics.

There is putting too much time in a thing to try. That is why you consult experts. Generally, after 2 years of really hard trying, it may be time for something else.

Mastermind Groups and Partners

Look at every major entertainer. Usher, for example, he is the front man on stage at the concert. He may be in a concert with 10 other artists, each with a group of backup dancers, pyrotechnics, stagehands, management, sponsors, crew, promoters, costume makers, designers, lighting crew, DJ's, photographers, sound specialist, security, and a slew of people that make sure he has a great show.

This is only one example. No one can become super great all by themselves.

Many of the super greats form associations with other greats. Henry Ford's best friend was Thomas Edison. Even in great history association of rivals have led to greatness. Like, John D. Rockefeller and Andrew Carnegie. Their relationship was a long one of "one-upping" each other. They were trying to each become the richest man alive, but later in their older years they caught the philanthropy bug and had a battle of charity giving much of their wealth away.

There is an old saying that no man is an island. The greatest country in the world is the United States. A country that by nature is divided, but unified by something bigger.

The whole is more than the sum of its parts.
Those that think if you want something right you need to do it yourself may become successful. But only as long as they are working hard at it. Usually, if they have to stop due to injury, illness or death that success usually falls with them.

I know how it can be with these type of people. Once I had a manager that had this attitude. She would push people aside to get the task done faster or more correct. Many times are clearing out a whole line of people. This would make the line of people angry and resentful. I would always say to her and everyone, that she was perfect, and you cannot improve on perfection! This, of course, was great sarcasm due to when we got busy we all would just point and laugh at her because she would not keep up with the timed pace that was already difficult to do with a team of people. She eventually got so far behind that her supervisor would take note of her attitude. She eventually could not work with too many people and later did not work there anymore.

Loyalty
You need to combine a different type of people like an introvert working with an extrovert. People that complement each other. People that can work well together.

Today many people can make connections on social media.

Note: Sometimes people betray you. Ask any major player. I'll bet they have a story of a bad business partner, manager, company, or even family. You should not be sleeping with one eye open, but you don't need to dismiss the possibility.

Set up security measures in place upon any problem. Sometimes the betrayal is not even meant, but it just happens. Such as a death of a partner and the relatives know nothing of the deal and screw up long term plans. You cannot do things by yourself.

I follow Troy Flora on twitter and tumbler, Tai Lopez on Facebook, and King Human on YouTube and more.

Henry Ford and Thomas Edison were great friends and helped each other out. There was one time when Thomas Edison had a fire in his home office. He had decades of inventions, research, and notes including his home. Thomas Edison was devastated as the firefighters were trying to put out the fire. He called his friend Henry Ford who rushed over while the fire was still burning. Thomas Edison said all of my life was in there! And now it is all over! Henry Ford wrote a check for 1 million dollars, a great deal back then. And he gave it to Thomas Edison, and said, it wasn't all lost in the fire, you made it out. You have much of the notes in your head; this money will help you to continue your life's work! If you need more, just let me know.

Planners Get More than Non-Planners

Change your mindset to avoid failures.

Don't just create a plan, create a system of plans.

Plan for best case scenario.
Plan for the worst case scenario.
Plan for the most likely scenario.

You need to look at all areas.

Write down your questions first.

Then write down your best 3 or more. Plans as a solution.

You then implement the most effective solution.

Things you can do is get a notebook or a day planner. Many smart devices and computers have a planner. This can help you keep track of all aspect of your plan.

This is one of the key steps of a highly effective person. Writing things down and keeping track. In the older days, people had to balance a checkbook. Everything pending, coming and going was on the back of a checkbook. Even card transactions and pending items were written down and accounted for.

Note: Currently banks depend on their account holders not keeping track. Not checking and not knowing pending transactions. This way they can make more money charging overdraft fees, and more.

Simply by writing down all of your finances at the time of purchase will help you keep track. It will be on your mind, and you will be mindful of frivolous spending.

This is one of the habits of a highly effective person.

Not just for money, meetings, planning, and also actions (that were and needed to be) taken.

There are 3 Factors to Good Production

1. Where you stand- Your location, and your contact.

This could be location, location, location. Put yourself where the traffic is for your customers. Tai Lopez talks about land. But if it is an online business which is a growing norm that just means your digital address. If you want to sell books, sell on Amazon because they are the largest retailer online for books. If you sell locally maybe craigslist is for you.

2. Labor- Your work knowledge and skill. Even if it is a one-man operation. You need to look for things like management, and how to use the tools you have. Any business person needs these skills even if they are a one-man show. If they want to grow their company they need to expand to other people for parts, labor, investments, knowledge, and support.

3. Capital- Financial to pay for it (money). You can learn about money and make it grow and work for you. If you do not have money, you may need investors. Many startups use the small business administration or kick starter and other programs like that to get off the ground.

You need to know your business

A summary of a story of Ray Crock from McDonald's. One-day Ray was in a bar just after a conference at a college. He asked some of the students there what his business was. One man said to him, "Come on Ray everybody knows that you sell hamburgers." Ray told them that it is true that he sells hamburgers, but that was not his primary business. He then told them that his primary business was not hamburgers but real estate. Today McDonald's owns some of the most attractive real estates around. They have locations on the right side of the road leaving town, and entering town from all major highways in countries where they drive on the right side of the road, and vice versa on the left side corners on countries where they drive on the left side of the road.

He then continued with the McDonald's business plan stated that they usually do 3 things that give them profit.

1. They own the land and having a long-term lease on the rental of that land for that location.

2. They sell franchise rights to the location- that the franchisees pay a fee every month/year for the use of the McDonald's system.

3. And last they sell food and get a percentage of every item sold.

Not bad.

The story of the guy talking to Ray Crock got the idea to open up car washes. He made a lot of money from that. He liked the idea of setting up a system that he did not have to monitor much.

Even that business is not one that you can just leave alone; you still need to check on it.

Reference page.

https://en.wikipedia.org/wiki/Google as seen 7/17/2016

Les Brown - You Gotta be Hungry [Les Brown Greatest Speech] Published on Jul 12, 2014

The Big Idea with Donny Deutsch, Published on Feb 16, 2014, Cilbup Oediv

Quotes from Famous People.

Jeanette Ellul, https://www.facebook.com/Uplifting-Thoughts-1631336490469377/
"Google - Wikipedia, the free encyclopedia." Insert Name of Site in Italics. N.p., n.d. Web. 17 Jul. 2016
<https://en.wikipedia.org/wiki/Google!>.

Steve Jobs explains the rules for success; https://youtu.be/KuNQgln6TL0

Uploaded on Sep 14, 2009, You need a lot of passion for what you're doing because it's so hard. Without passion, any rational person would give up. So if you're not having fun doing it, if you don't love it, you're going to give up. And that's what happens to most people. Viewed 10/9/2015. Where he was together with bill gates.

The One Minute Millionaire: The Enlightened Way to Wealth by Mark Victor Hansen, Robert G. Allen, Crown Publishing Group, 2009

Cash in a Flash: Real Money in No Time, Crown Business
Dec 28, 2010, by Robert G. Allen and Mark Victor Hansen

Managing Oneself (Harvard Business Review Classics) 1st Edition, Publisher: Harvard Business Press; 1 edition (January 7, 2008), Language: English, ISBN-10: 142212312X, ISBN-13: 978-1422123126.

Jay the lazy ass stoner on YouTube.com as seen 1-1-1016

MLA: "HOW TO GET THINGS DONE? Accomplish!" Insert Name of Site in Italics. N.p., n.d. Web. 17 Jul. 2016
<http://www.thepreparedperformer.com/how-to-get-things-done-actually-accomplish/>.

www.ingramcontent.com/pod-product-compliance
Lightning Source LLC
Chambersburg PA
CBHW071203220526
45468CB00003B/1140